# WHAT IS POISON?

## Poison is a substance that hurts or kills a living thing.

Many animals and bugs are born with *poison* in their bodies. This poison is called *venom*. The animals use the venom to kill prey or defend themselves. A creature that does this is *venomous* (VEN-um-iss).

Venomous animals use special body parts to deliver poison. They may have fangs, a stinger, *tentacles*, or a strawlike beak called a *proboscis* (pro-BOS-iss). Some venom hurts the heart or lungs. Other venom harms the blood.

# LAND ANIMALS

In this book, you will learn about some **venomous creatures**.

You will find out where they live, what they eat, and how big they grow. Get ready to explore the world of poison!

# FAST FACTS

**Venomous** animals have poison in their bodies and *inject* it into their prey. **Poisonous** animals have poison in their bodies, but they can't deliver it. An animal that eats a poisonous creature, like a toad, will become sick or even die.

Trapdoor Spider

Numbers:
hundreds of
different kinds

Where found:
all over the
world

Mangrove Snake

All of these animals live on land. Most live
on the ground all the time. Others are found
in trees and in the water, too! About ⅓ of all
the animals in the world live on land.

# GILA MONSTER

*(Heloderma suspectum)*

- ◎ Gila monsters are the only venomous lizards found in the United States.

- ◎ The Gila monster puts venom into its victim by biting it with sharp teeth. As the Gila monster chews, it injects even more venom!

- ◎ Gila monsters can go for months without food. They live off of fat stored in their tail.

# FAST FACTS

**Length:** 18 to 22 inches (46 to 55 cm)

**Weight:** about 3 pounds (1.3 kg)

**Color:** black, pink, and yellow beadlike, scaly skin

**Food:** small *mammals*, birds, lizards, frogs, and eggs

**Where found:** deserts in Mexico and the United States

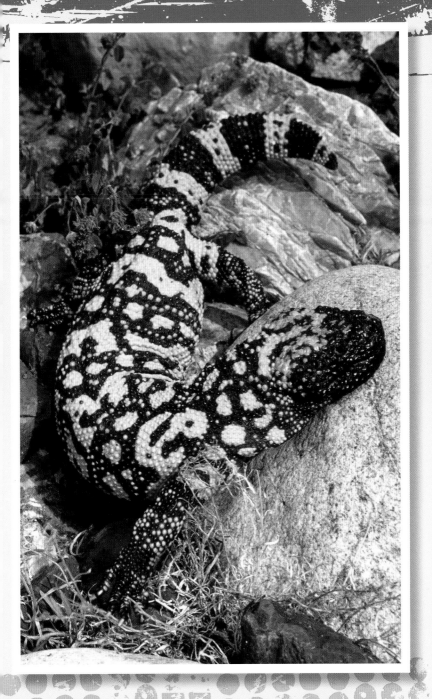

# MONITOR LIZARDS

## (Varanus)

◎ Monitor lizards are related to the mosasaur (MOH-suh-sawr). The mosasaur lived during the time of the dinosaurs.

◎ A monitor lizard has a long, forked tongue and a powerful tail.

◎ Monitor lizards inject venom by biting their victims with sharp teeth.

The largest monitor lizard is the Komodo dragon. It can weigh up to 365 pounds (165 kg)!

# FAST FACTS

**Length:** 8 inches to 13 feet (20 cm to 4 m)

**Color:** many different colors

**Food:** small mammals, reptiles, reptile eggs, birds, insects, and *carrion* (dead animals)

**Where found:** Africa, Asia, East Indies, and Australia

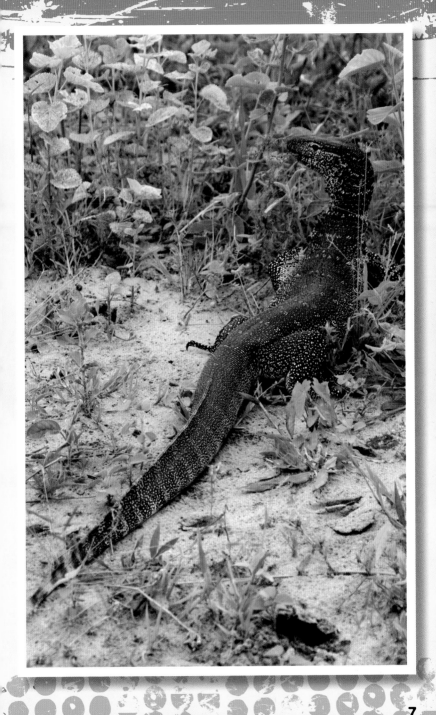

# RATTLESNAKE

## (Crotalus, Sistrurus)

- ◎ Rattlesnakes have long fangs. They use the fangs to inject venom into their prey.

- ◎ An adult rattlesnake eats about every two weeks.

- ◎ Rattlesnakes are pit vipers. They have holes (pits) on their head that sense the body heat of their prey.

# FAST FACTS

**Length:** 1 foot to 8 feet (0.3 to 2.4 m)

**Color:** many different shades and patterns of brown

**Food:** rabbits, squirrels, mice, rats, frogs, and lizards

**Where found:** North, Central, and South America

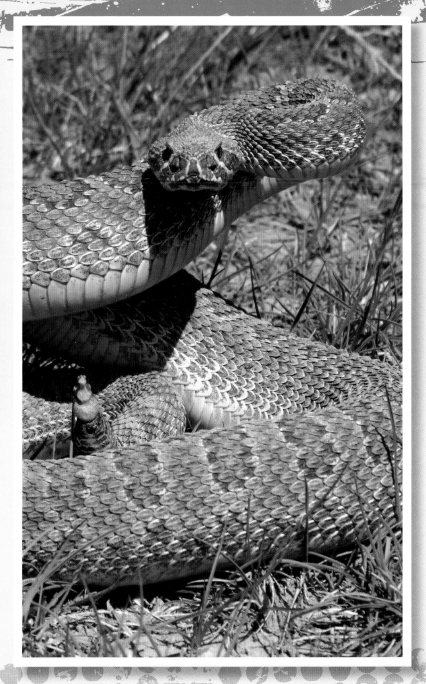

# BLACK MAMBA

## (Dendroaspis polylepsis)

◎ Black mambas are the fastest moving snakes in the world. They can travel 12½ miles per hour (20 kph).

◎ The black mamba injects venom into its prey using sharp fangs.

◎ When a black mamba gets scared, it can raise its body and head 4 feet (1.2 m) off the ground.

The black mamba gets its name from the black color on the inside of its mouth.

# FAST FACTS

**Length:** 14 feet (4.5 m)

**Color:** gray or olive green

**Food:** mice, squirrels, birds, frogs, and lizards

**Where found:** Africa

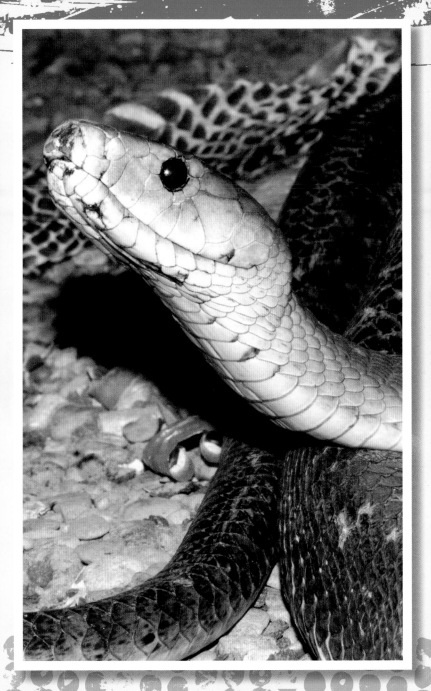

# INLAND TAIPAN

## (Oxyuranus microlepidotus)

◎ The inland taipan is the most venomous
land snake in the world.

◎ Inland taipans inject venom with long,
sharp fangs.

◎ Like all snakes, the inland taipan keeps
growing its entire life.

# FAST FACTS

**Length:** 6½ feet (2 m)

**Color:** dark tan or brownish olive-green

**Food:** small rodents (mainly rats)

**Where found:** Australia

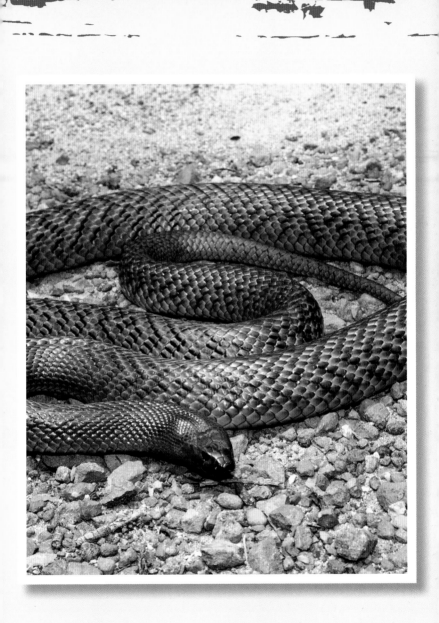

# COPPERHEAD

## *(Agkistrodon contortrix)*

◎ When copperheads sense danger, they stop moving. They stay motionless until the threat passes.

◎ A copperhead puts venom into its victim by biting it with long fangs.

◎ A female copperhead can lay as many as 20 eggs at a time.

# FAST FACTS

**Length:** 2 to 3 feet (0.6 to 0.9 m)

**Color:** copper with darker bands

**Food:** mice, voles, frogs, lizards, birds, and bugs

**Where found:** United States and Mexico

# KING COBRA

*(Ophiophagus hannah)*

◎ King cobras have fangs that don't fold up into the snake's mouth. They bite their prey with the fangs to inject venom.

◎ The king cobra is the longest venomous snake. Some are as long as a car!

◎ These snakes are excellent swimmers.

# FAST FACTS

**Length:** 13 to 18 feet (4 to 5.5 m)

**Color:** yellow, green, brown, or black; light yellow throat

**Food:** other snakes, lizards, rodents, and birds

**Where found:** India, southern China, and Southeast Asia

# MANGROVE SNAKE

*(Boiga dendrophila)*

- ◎ The mangrove snake has small fangs in the back of its mouth. The snake bites its victim to inject venom.

- ◎ Mangrove snakes are good swimmers.

- ◎ Mangrove snakes are also known as yellow-ringed cat snakes.

# FAST FACTS

**Length:** 6 to 8 feet (1.8 to 2.4 m)

**Color:** black with yellow bands

**Food:** birds and bird eggs, frogs, rodents, bats, and other snakes

**Where found:** Southeast Asia and India

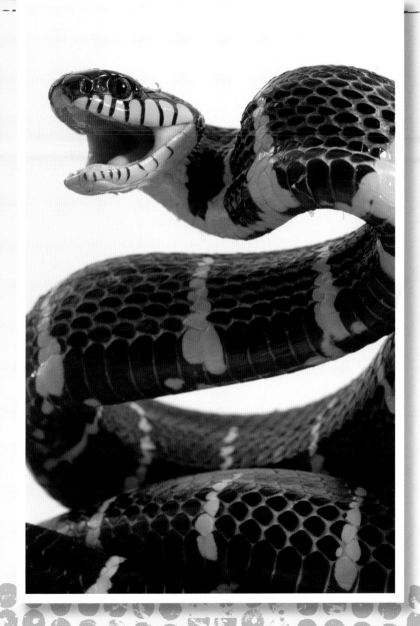

# CORAL SNAKE

## (Leptomicrurus micrurus)

- ◎ Coral snakes belong to the same family as cobras.

- ◎ A coral snake bites its prey with small fangs to inject venom.

- ◎ Coral snakes are *nocturnal*. This mean they are active at night.

# FAST FACTS

**Length:** 2 feet (0.6 m)

**Color:** black, yellow, and red bands

**Food:** other snakes, rats, mice, and lizards

**Where found:** all over the world

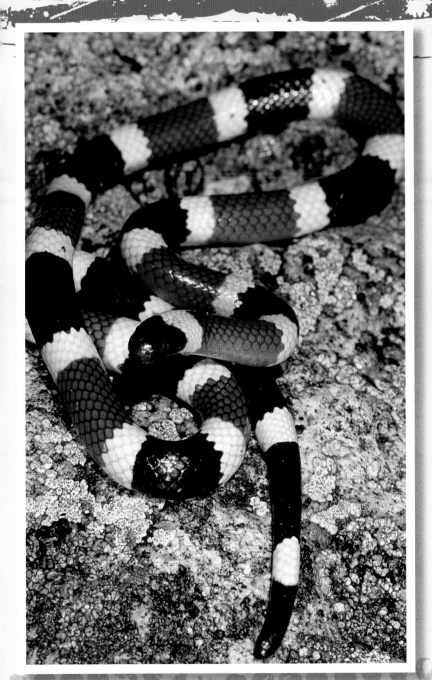

# GREEN BAMBOO VIPER

## (*Trimeresurus stejnegeri*)

◎ This snake delivers poison with long fangs.

◎ It moves slowly, but is very aggressive.

◎ Green bamboo vipers have red eyes.

# FAST FACTS

**Length:** 20 to 30 inches (50 to 76 cm)

**Color:** green with a red tail

**Food:** rodents, lizards, and birds

**Where found:** Southeast China, Thailand, Vietnam, India, and Taiwan

# BLACK WIDOW SPIDER

## (Latrodectus)

◎ Black widow spiders put venom into their prey by biting it with their fangs.

◎ Drop for drop, a black widow's venom is stronger than a rattlesnake's venom.

◎ Only female black widows are dangerous to humans. Males and young black widows are harmless.

# FAST FACTS

**Length:** ¾ inch to 1½ inches (2 to 3.8 cm)

**Color:** shiny black body; females have a red hourglass shape on their belly

**Food:** insects

**Where found:** warm parts of the world

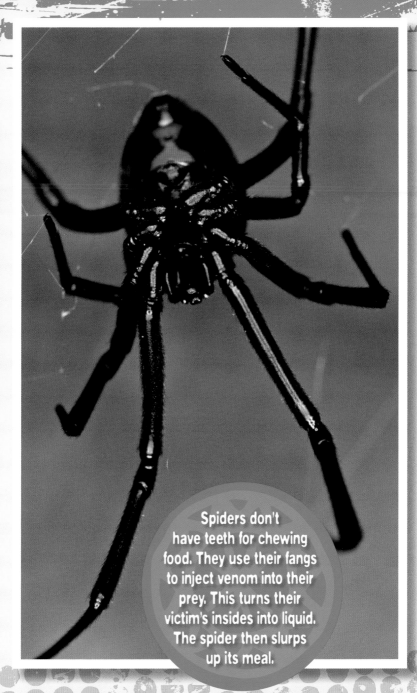

Spiders don't have teeth for chewing food. They use their fangs to inject venom into their prey. This turns their victim's insides into liquid. The spider then slurps up its meal.

# SYDNEY FUNNEL-WEB SPIDER

*(Atrax robustus)*

- The Sydney funnel-web is the most dangerous spider in the world to humans. A single bite can kill if the wound is not treated.

- This spider uses its long fangs to inject venom into prey.

- The Sydney funnel-web lives in a hole under rocks or logs. It puts silk lines outside the hole to catch prey. The victim trips on the silk line. Then, the spider rushes out of the hole to grab its meal.

# FAST FACTS

**Length:** ½ inch to 1½ inches (1.3 to 3.8 cm)

**Color:** shiny dark brown or black

**Food:** small lizards, snails, beetles, and cockroaches

**Where found:** Australia

# GOLIATH BIRD EATER

## (Theraphosa blondi)

- ◎ Goliath bird eaters are tarantulas (hairy spiders). They are the largest tarantulas in the world.

- ◎ These spiders rarely eat birds, but they are big enough to do so!

- ◎ The Goliath bird eater kills its victim by injecting venom with its fangs.

## FAST FACTS

**Length:** 12-inch (30-cm) leg span

**Weight:** 2½ ounces (70 g)

**Color:** light and dark brown

**Food:** frogs, small snakes, lizards, beetles, insects, bats, and birds

**Where found:** South America

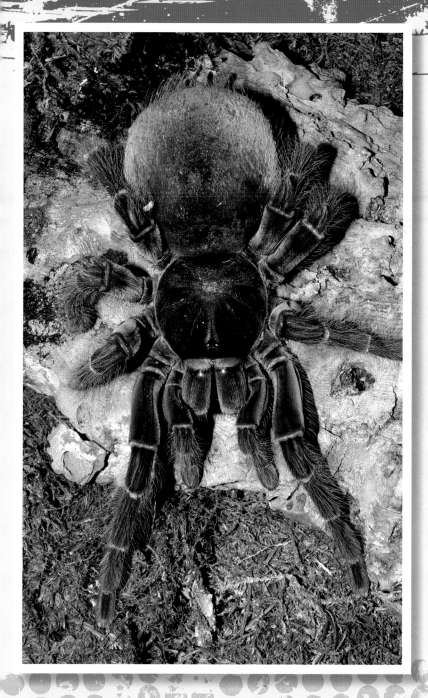

# TRAPDOOR SPIDER

## (Ctenizidae)

◎ A trapdoor spider lives in a *burrow* (a hole in the ground). It covers the burrow with dirt, grass, and silk to make a trap door. When prey comes by, the spider grabs it.

◎ These spiders inject venom into their prey by biting it with their fangs.

◎ There are 120 different kinds of trapdoor spiders.

# FAST FACTS

**Length:** ¼ to ¾ inch (6.5 to 19 mm)

**Color:** black or brown with spotty markings

**Food:** small birds, small snakes, mice, small fish, frogs, and insects

**Where found:** Africa, Japan, South America, and North America

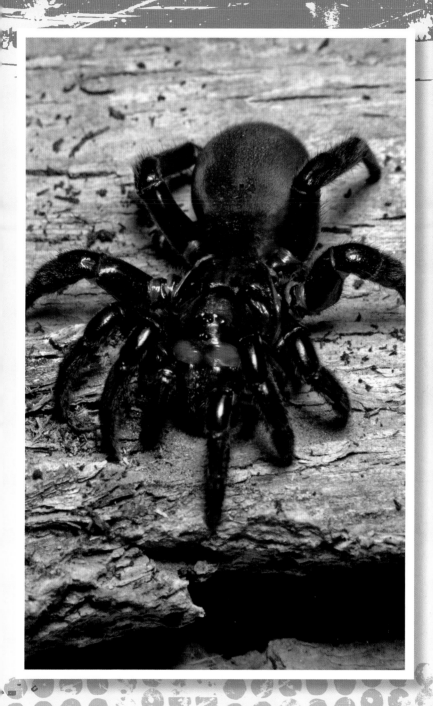

# BROWN RECLUSE SPIDER

*(Loxosceles reclusa)*

- ◎ Most spiders have four pairs of eyes. The brown recluse has three pairs.

- ◎ Brown recluse spiders inject venom into their prey with tiny fangs.

- ◎ The brown recluse spider lives in small, dark places.

# FAST FACTS

**Length:** ¼ to ¾ inch (6.5 to 19 mm)

**Color:** golden brown with a dark-brown or black fiddle shape on the head

**Food:** insects

**Where found:** United States

# WOLF SPIDER

## (Lycosidae)

◎ There are more than 2,000 different kinds of wolf spiders in the world.

◎ The wolf spider hunts its prey by running after it.

◎ Wolf spiders have fangs. They bite their victims to inject venom.

# FAST FACTS

**Length:** ⅛ inch to 3 inches (1 to 8 cm)

**Color:** dark brown

**Food:** insects and other spiders

**Where found:** all over the world

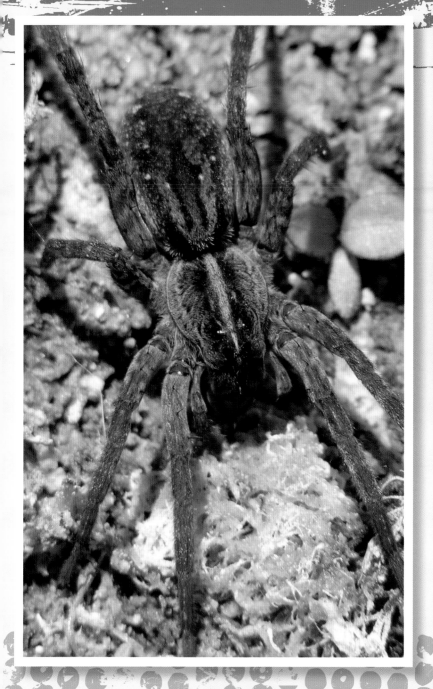

# DADDY LONG-LEGS SPIDER

*(Pholcus phalangioides)*

- ◎ Daddy longlegs spiders inject venom with short fangs.

- ◎ After the female lays her eggs, she wraps them in silk and carries them in her jaws until they hatch.

- ◎ This spider is almost see-through. If you use a microscope, you can see the blood cells moving in its body!

# FAST FACTS

**Length:** ¼ to ⅓ inch (6 to 8 mm)

**Color:** pale yellow-brown with a gray patch on the head and *thorax*

**Food:** insects and other spiders

**Where found:** all over the world

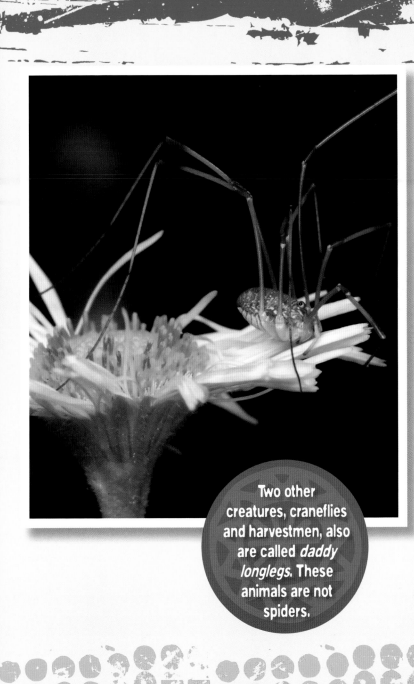

Two other creatures, craneflies and harvestmen, also are called *daddy longlegs*. These animals are not spiders.

# BULLET ANT
## (Paraponera clevata)

◎ Bullet ants deliver poison with a stinger. The sting is extremely painful.

◎ If these ants bite something too hard to be crushed by their jaws, the force hurls them into the air!

◎ When a bullet ant bites, its jaws spring shut at more then 60 miles per hour (97 kph).

# FAST FACTS

**Length:** 1 inch (2.5 cm)

**Color:** reddish-black

**Food:** insects (mainly termites) and flower *nectar*

**Where found:** rain forests in Central and South America

# CENTIPEDE

*(Chilopoda)*

- ◎ Centipedes are nocturnal.

- ◎ A centipede injects venom into its victim with its fangs.

- ◎ Centipedes are the only insects that have fangs.

The word *centipede* means "one hundred feet." Many centipedes have fewer than that. Some have more!

# FAST FACTS

**Length:** 1 inch to 3 feet (2.5 cm to 1 m)

**Color:** pale yellow to dark brown

**Food:** spiders, slugs, earthworms, and insects

**Where found:** warm parts of the world

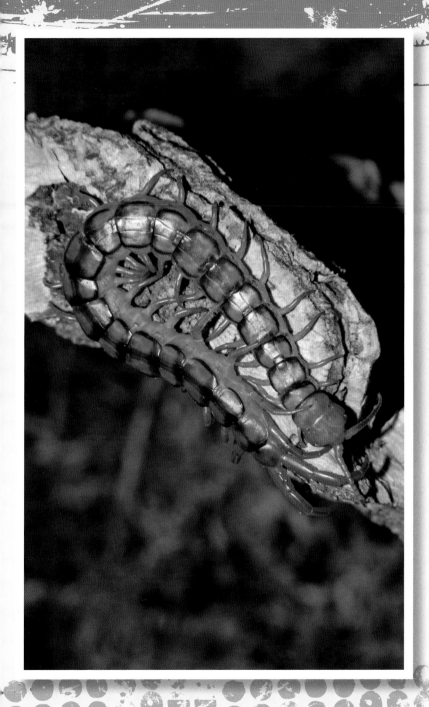

# DEATH STALKER SCORPION

*(Leiurus quinquestriatus)*

- ◎ Death stalkers are the most venomous scorpions on Earth.

- ◎ The death stalker delivers venom with a stinger at the tip of its tail.

- ◎ Death stalkers hunt at night.

# FAST FACTS

**Length:** 3½ to 4½ inches (9 to 11.5 cm)

**Color:** tan or reddish-brown with a black stinger and pincer tips

**Food:** spiders, crickets, flies, and moths

**Where found:** deserts in northern Africa and the Middle East

# PUSS MOTH CATERPILLAR

### (Megalopyge opercularis)

◎ The puss moth caterpillar injects venom through hollow hairs. The hairs are attached to poison sacs on its body.

◎ The puss moth is one of the most *toxic* caterpillars in North America.

◎ Puss moth caterpillars can sting even after they're dead! The venom in the hollow hairs still can be injected into a person's skin if the caterpillar is picked up.

# FAST FACTS

**Length:** 1 inch to 1½ inches (2.5 to 3.8 cm)

**Color:** brown, tan, or gray

**Food:** plants, trees, leaves, and shrubs

**Where found:** southern United States and Mexico

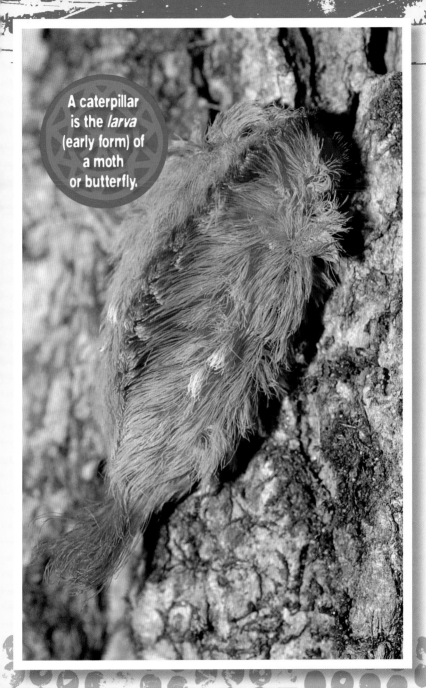

A caterpillar is the *larva* (early form) of a moth or butterfly.

# SADDLEBACK CATERPILLAR

## (Sibine stimulea)

- ◎ The saddleback caterpillar has horns on its front and back ends.

- ◎ A saddleback injects venom through hollow hairs. The hairs are attached to poison sacs on the caterpillar's body.

- ◎ The front and back ends of saddleback caterpillars look the same. This makes it hard for *predators* to know where to attack.

# FAST FACTS

**Length:** 1 inch (2.5 cm)

**Color:** purplish-brown body with a green saddle shape on the back; dark purple spot in the middle of the "saddle"

**Food:** tree and shrub leaves

**Where found:** eastern North America

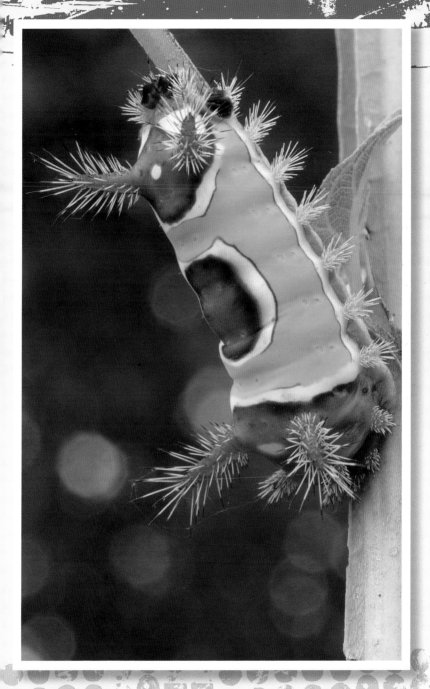

# PLATYPUS

## (Ornithorhynchus anatinus)

- Scientists studying the platypus have discovered that the platypus is a strange combination of mammal, reptile, and bird.

- This unique animal has a bill like a duck, a tail like a beaver, and feet like an otter.

- The male platypus has a spike on his hind foot. The spike is used to inject venom, usually in self-defense or when fighting other males.

# FAST FACTS

**Length:** 16 to 24 inches (41 to 61 cm)

**Weight:** 2 to 5 pounds (0.9 to 2 kg)

**Color:** waterproof dark brown fur; gray-blue bill

**Food:** shrimp, snails, crayfish, insects, and worms

**Where found:** Australia

# SLOW LORIS

**(Nycticebus coucang)**

- ◎ Slow lorises have venom in the glands of their inner elbows. They mix this venom with their saliva. Then, they deliver the venom by biting.

- ◎ The venom has a strong, unpleasant odor. Mothers cover their babies with the venom to keep predators away.

- ◎ Slow lorises are *arboreal* (are-bore-E-al). This means they live in trees.

# FAST FACTS

**Length:** 8 to 15 inches (21 to 38 cm)

**Weight:** about 4½ pounds (2 kg)

**Color:** brown or reddish-brown fur

**Food:** small mammals, baby birds, bird eggs, insects, and fruit

**Where found:** Southeast Asia

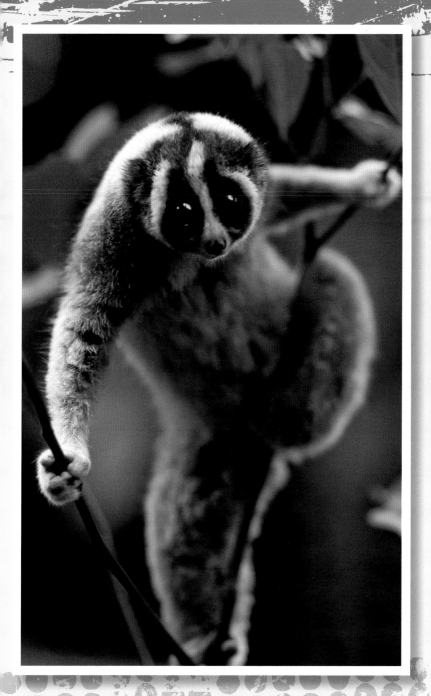

# SHORT-TAILED SHREW
### (Blarina)

◎ Short-tailed shrews need to eat their weight in food every day.

◎ These animals are good diggers and swimmers.

◎ Short-tailed shrews have venom in the glands of their lower jaw. This venom mixes with their saliva. They deliver the venom by biting.

# FAST FACTS

**Length:** 3½ inches (8.8 cm)

**Weight:** less than 1 ounce (14 g)

**Color:** gray-brown fur

**Food:** mice, lizards, worms, snails, insects, nuts, and berries

**Where found:** United States and Canada

# SEA ANIMALS

## There are animals in the sea that have venom, too.

Venomous creatures include jellyfish, octopuses, and certain fish. Some, like sea snakes, live where it's warm. Others, like the Arctic jellyfish, live where it's cold.

Numbers:
about 1,000 different kinds of venomous fish

9,000 different kinds of venomous *invertebrates* (animals without a backbone)

Where found:
in waters all over the world

**Portuguese Man-of-War**

- The most venomous animal on Earth lives in the sea. It's the box jellyfish.

- Many sea creatures use venom to defend themselves or to hunt prey.

- Sea creatures release their poison by touching (like a Portuguese man-of-war) or injecting (like a snake).

- Venomous sea creatures usually don't attack unless they get scared.

Stinging Coral

# BOX JELLYFISH

**(also called a *sea wasp* and a *marine stinger*)**
**(*Chironex fleckeri*)**

◎ The venom of the box jellyfish is the deadliest in the animal kingdom.

◎ Sea turtles are not hurt by the box jellyfish's sting. The turtles eat the jellyfish!

◎ The box jellyfish has 60 tentacles that can grow to be 15 feet (4.5 m) long.

◎ The body is large and shaped like a box.

Box jellyfish have up to 5,000 stinging cells on their tentacles. The cells shoot out like darts.

# FAST FACTS

**Length:** the bell (body) can get as big as a basketball

**Color:** clear pale blue

**Food:** small fish and shellfish

**Where found:** Australia, the Philippines, and tropical seas

# BLUE-RINGED OCTOPUS

## (Hapalochlaena)

◎ There are about 10 different kinds of blue-ringed octopus.

◎ The venom is made by bacteria in the octopus's saliva.

◎ Octopuses live for only about two years.

◎ The blue-ringed octopus has green blood, three hearts, and eight arms.

# FAST FACTS

**Length:** 4½ to 6 inches (12 to 15 cm)

**Color:** *camouflaged* until scared, then it turns yellow with blue rings or lines

**Food:** small crabs and shrimp

**Where found:** tidal pools in Japan and Australia

# STONEFISH

*(Synanceia verrucosa)*

- The stonefish lives on the bottom of the reef bed.

- Stonefish have venomous spines on their back.

- It's the most venomous fish.

# FAST FACTS

**Length:** 13½ to 19½ inches (35 to 50 cm)

**Color:** camouflaged, many different colors

**Food:** small fish and shrimp

**Where found:** coral reefs in the Pacific and Indian Oceans

# SEA SNAKES

## (Elapidae)

◎ Sea snakes breathe air.

◎ The flat tail of the sea snake helps it to swim.

◎ Sea snakes can stay underwater for a few hours.

◎ These snakes have short fangs and very toxic venom.

The most venomous sea snake is the beaded sea snake.

# FAST FACTS

**Length:** 4 to 5 feet (1.2 to 1.5 m)

**Color:** many different colors and patterns

**Food:** fish, fish eggs, and eels

**Where found:** warm, shallow waters in the Indian and Pacific Oceans

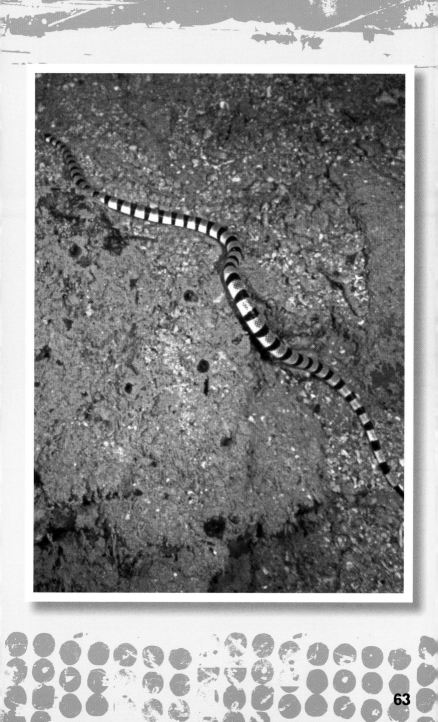

# STINGRAY

## (Dasyatidae)

- Stingrays are a type of fish. They are related to sharks.

- Rays move their wings to glide through the water.

- The stinger is a razor-sharp spine that grows at the end of the tail.

- Stingrays bury themselves in the sand to hide and hunt for prey.

# FAST FACTS

**Length:** 5 inches to 6½ feet (12.5 cm to 2 m)

**Color:** gray and brown; some have patterns

**Food:** fish, fish eggs, and eels

**Where found:** Atlantic, Pacific, and Indian Oceans

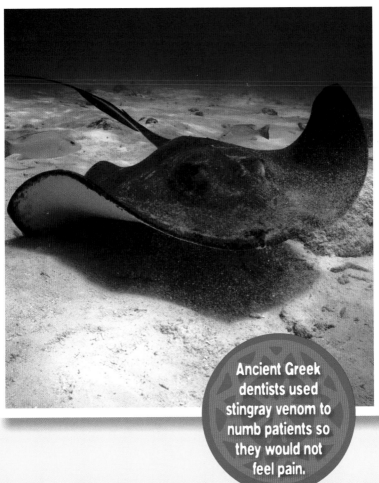

Ancient Greek dentists used stingray venom to numb patients so they would not feel pain.

# PUFFERFISH

## (Tetraodontidae)

◎ Its skin and some internal organs are poisonous to humans.

◎ Pufferfish swim very slowly.

◎ The pufferfish can move each eye separately.

◎ A pufferfish can look like a big balloon by filling its stomach with water.

# FAST FACTS

**Length:** up to 20 inches (51 cm)

**Color:** bright colors in many different patterns

**Food:** algae, seaweed, clams, shrimp, scallops, and mussels

**Where found:** near the shore, from the Atlantic Ocean to the Pacific Ocean

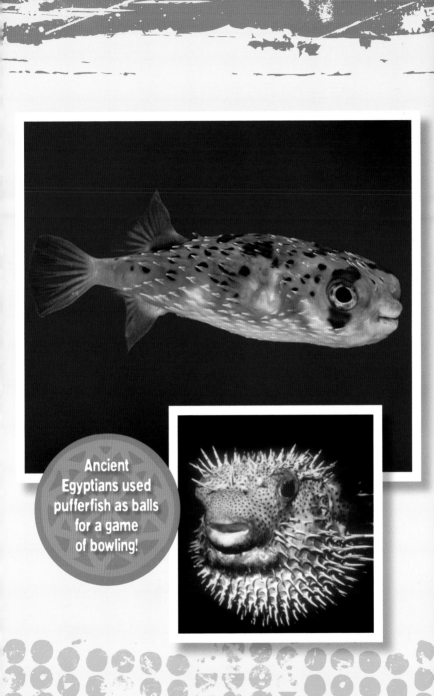

Ancient Egyptians used pufferfish as balls for a game of bowling!

# SEA URCHIN

## (Toxopneustes pileolus)

- ◎ Sea urchins hide in the holes in rocks during the day.

- ◎ Sea urchins look like balls or biscuits.

- ◎ They move by using their spines or tube feet.

- ◎ The sting of the flower urchin is very poisonous.

# FAST FACTS

**Length:** 1 inch to 4 inches (3 to 10 cm)

**Color:** usually black, but can be purple, brown, or white

**Food:** kelp and *plankton*

**Where found:** in every ocean around the world

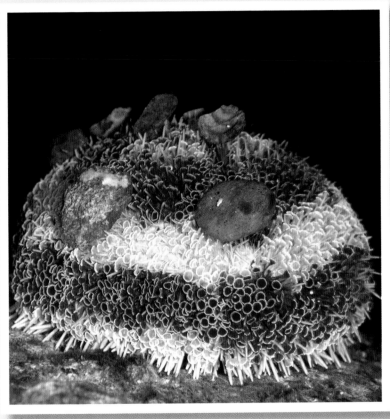

# CONE SNAIL

## *(Conidae)*

◎ There are more than 500 different kinds of cone snails.

◎ Cone snails move very slowly.

◎ A cone snail uses its venomous tongue with a harpoonlike tip to catch prey.

◎ Cone snails suck up water to smell prey.

# FAST FACTS

**Length:** up to 6 inches (15 cm)

**Color:** usually brown and white patterned shells

**Food:** *marine* worms, small fish, mollusks, and other cone snails

**Where found:** reefs in the Indian and Pacific Oceans

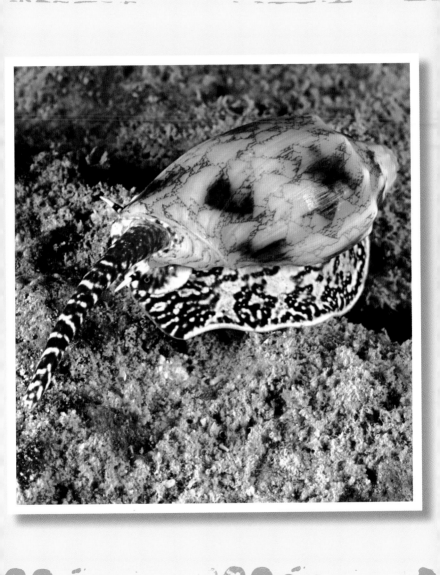

# PORTUGUESE MAN-OF-WAR

**(Physalia physalis)**

◎ Man-of-wars have an air bladder. This allows them to float on the ocean's surface.

◎ The venom is located on the tentacles.

◎ Portuguese man-of-wars are not jellyfish.

Its tentacles can reach 33 feet (10 m) in length!

# FAST FACTS

**Length:** up to 170 feet (52 m)

**Color:** purplish-blue

**Food:** small fish and shrimp

**Where found:** warm waters throughout the world, and in the North Atlantic Gulf Stream

# SCORPIONFISH

## (Scorpaenidae)

◎ Scorpionfish have venomous spines all over their bodies.

◎ Some scorpionfish can change color to blend in with their surroundings. This is called camouflage.

◎ There are more than 1,000 different kinds of scorpionfish.

# FAST FACTS

**Length:** up to 20 inches (51 cm)

**Color:** many different bright colors

**Food:** small fish

**Where found:** rocks and reefs of warm oceans; mostly found in the Pacific and Indian Oceans

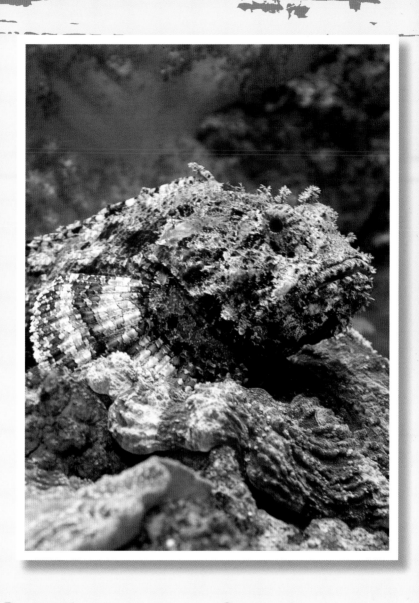

# TOADFISH

**(Opsanus tau)**

◉ Male toadfish "sing" to attract a female.

◉ A toadfish has hollow spines along its back and tail fin. The fish injects venom through the spines.

◉ Toadfish can live out of water for short periods of time.

# FAST FACTS

**Length:** about 1 foot (0.3 m)

**Color:** usually olive green, brown, or dull yellow

**Food:** fish, shrimp, and other small marine animals

**Where found:** near the bottom of waters along the coast of North America

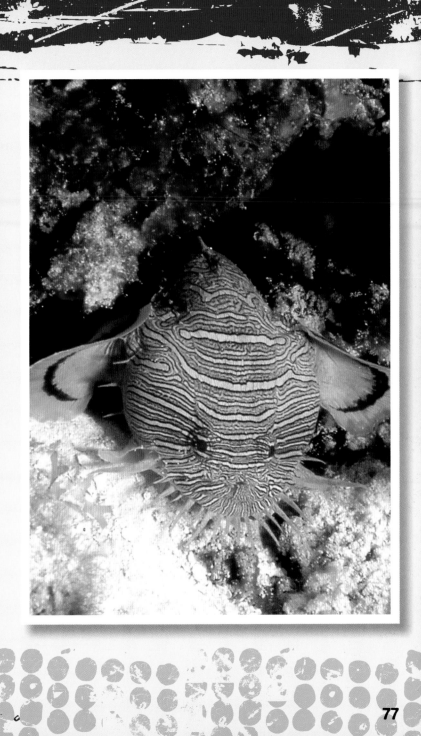

# LIONFISH

## (Scorpaenidae)

- ◎ The lionfish is a type of scorpionfish.

- ◎ Lionfish will eat anything that they can get in their mouths.

- ◎ These fish are found around reefs and rocky crevices.

- ◎ Lionfish hunt at night.

# FAST FACTS

**Length:** 12 to 15 inches (30 to 38 cm)

**Color:** red and white stripes

**Food:** fish and shrimp

**Where found:** warm oceans around the world

# SEA CUCUMBER

### (Holothuroidea)

- ◎ The sea cucumber has a soft, long body that looks like a cucumber.

- ◎ Sea cucumbers are found on the ocean floor.

- ◎ Sea cucumbers are related to starfish.

- ◎ These animals move by using small tubes on the bottom of their bodies.

# FAST FACTS

**Length:** ½ inch to 3½ feet (1.3 cm to 1 m)

**Color:** many different colors

**Food:** plankton

**Where found:** tropical reefs around the world

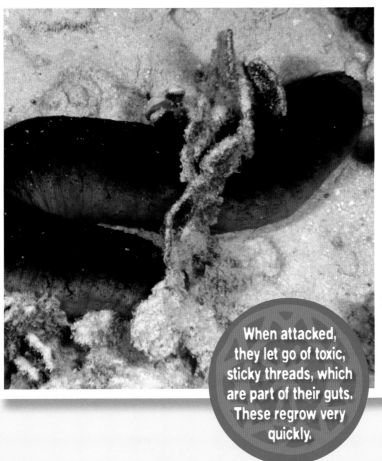

When attacked, they let go of toxic, sticky threads, which are part of their guts. These regrow very quickly.

# SEA ANEMONE

**(also called *the flower of the sea*)**

**(Actiniaria)**

◎ Sea anemones are related to jellyfish and corals.

◎ The sea anemone can have 10 to more than 100 tentacles.

◎ Sea anemones look like plants, but they are meat-eating animals.

◎ The sticky foot of the sea anemone attaches to rocks or coral.

# FAST FACTS

**Length:** ½ inch to 6 feet (1.25 cm to 2 m) in diameter

**Color:** many different colors

**Food:** small fish and shrimp

**Where found:** oceans all over the world, but mostly in warmer climates

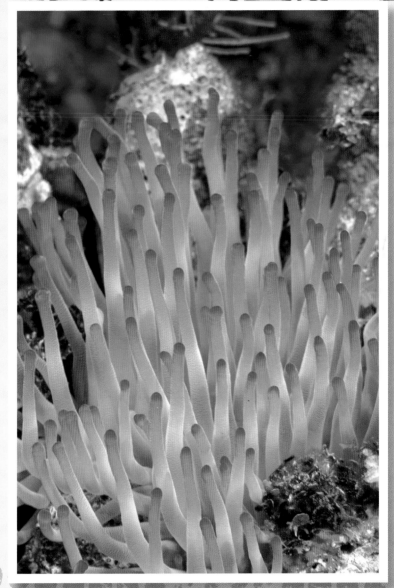

# STINGING CORAL

**(also called *fire coral*)**

**(*Millepora*)**

◎ Stinging coral look like coral, but are related to jellyfish and sea anemone.

◎ This coral has a delicate fan shape.

◎ Stinging coral deliver venom with very small tentacles.

Fire coral *colonies* can grow to be 5 feet (1.5 m).

# FAST FACTS

**Length:** each ⅛ inch to 2½ inches (3 to 56 mm) in diameter

**Color:** yellow, brown, red, white, orange, and green.

**Food:** plankton

**Where found:** Indian and Pacific Oceans

# CATFISH

## (Siluriformes)

- Catfish have a flat head. This allows them to dig for prey.

- These fish do not have scales.

- Most catfish have a bony, spinelike ray on their back and tail fin. The ray can deliver a nasty sting.

- The electric catfish of Africa can generate up to 350 volts of electricity.

# FAST FACTS

**Length:** ½ inch to 10 feet (10 mm to 3 m)

**Color:** gray, blue, dark green, brown, white, peach, or yellow

**Food:** crayfish, clams, worms, insect larvae, and small fish

**Where found:** saltwater and freshwater on every continent, except Antarctica

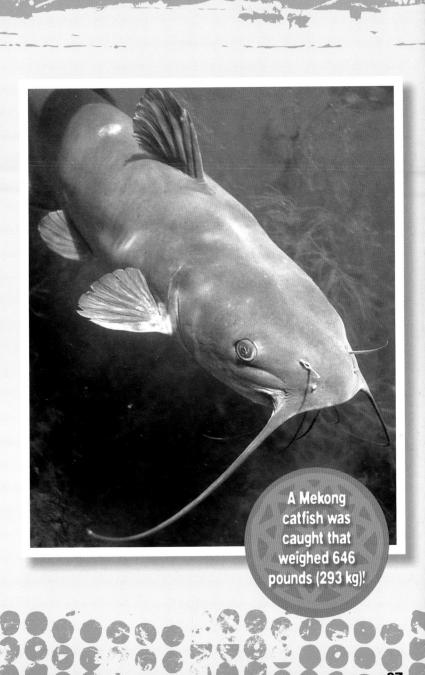

A Mekong catfish was caught that weighed 646 pounds (293 kg)!

# AIR ANIMALS

Some insects have venom in their bodies, too.
Insects have things in common with each other.

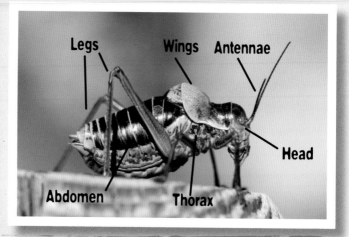

Legs   Wings   Antennae

Head

Abdomen   Thorax

- ◎ Insects have three body parts: head, thorax, and *abdomen*.

- ◎ Most have six legs.

- ◎ They have two antennae.

- ◎ Many have an *exoskeleton* (a hard covering on the outside of their body).

- ◎ Most have wings and can fly.

Insects are very important. Some, like bees, help flowers make seeds for fruit or new plants. Others, like assassin bugs, eat other insects that can be pests.

Numbers: more than one million different kinds

Where found: all over the world

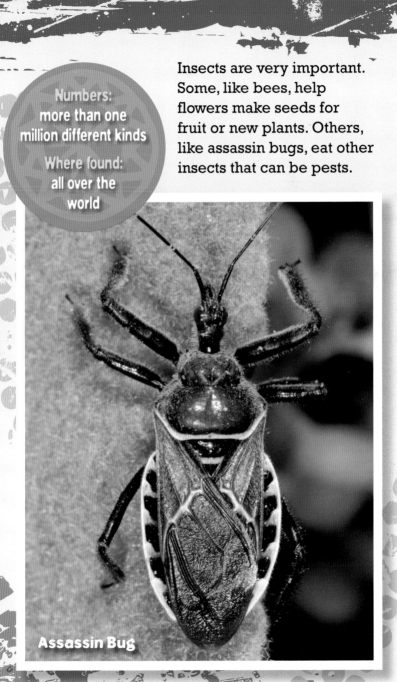

Assassin Bug

# WASP

## (Vespidae)

◎ Many wasps build nests made of mud. Some wasps chew plants to make a cone-shaped, paperlike nest.

◎ Female wasps have a stinger attached to a venom sac on their bodies. They deliver the venom by stinging.

◎ There are about 5,000 different species of wasps in the world. Hornets and yellow jackets are two kinds.

# FAST FACTS

**Length:** less than ½ inch to 2 inches (1.3 to 5 cm)

**Color:** all different colors

**Food:** fruit, flower nectar, insects, and carrion

**Where found:** all over the world

# HONEYBEE

## (Apis mellifera)

◎ Female honeybees have a stinger attached to a venom sac on their bodies. They deliver the venom by stinging.

◎ A honeybee leaves its stinger and part of its body when it stings.

◎ Bees "dance" to show other bees where to find nectar.

# FAST FACTS

**Length:** ⅖ to ⅝ inch (10 to 16 mm)

**Color:** golden brown and black

**Food:** flower nectar

**Where found:** all over the world

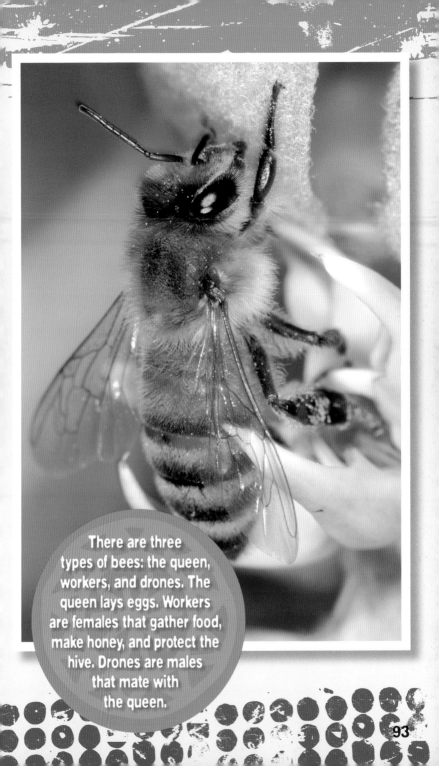

There are three types of bees: the queen, workers, and drones. The queen lays eggs. Workers are females that gather food, make honey, and protect the hive. Drones are males that mate with the queen.

# ASSASSIN BUG

## (Reduviidae)

◎ Assassin bugs are poor fliers.

◎ Assassin bugs have a proboscis , which is a strawlike beak. They stab their prey with the proboscis and inject venom. Then they slurp up their meal.

◎ If other food is not available, assassin bugs will eat each other.

# FAST FACTS

**Length:** up to 1½ inches (3.8 cm)

**Color:** gray, green, orange, brown, black, or a combination of these

**Food:** other insects

**Where found:** all over the world

# BUMBLEBEE

## (Bombus)

◎ Female bumblebees have a stinger attached to a venom sac on their bodies. They deliver the venom by stinging.

◎ Unlike honeybees, bumblebees can sting more than once.

◎ Sometimes, bumblebees build a wax "roof" over their hive for protection.

# FAST FACTS

**Length:** about ¾ inch (1.9 cm)

**Color:** fuzzy black and yellow hairs

**Food:** flower nectar

**Where found:** all over the world